Y0-AGR-422

Approaching Graz, Styria

C. Hamilton Ellis

Railway history

a dutton vista pictureback

General editor David Herbert

Wartime Russia

© C. Hamilton Ellis 1966
Published in London by Studio Vista Limited
Blue Star House, Highgate Hill, N 19
and in New York by E. P. Dutton and Co Inc
201 Park Avenue South, New York 3, NY
Set in 8D on 9 pt Univers, 2 pts leaded
Made and printed in Great Britain by
Richard Clay (The Chaucer Press), Ltd, Bungay, Suffolk

Contents

The very first railway locomotive (Richard Trevithick, 1804)

From the dark ages to 1830

Something very important happened in North-Western England on September 15, 1830. To many of those who watched it, this was simply an unusual spectacle. But even among the ordinary spectators, and in the intervals of dashing for cover from successive heavy downpours, there were some who knew they were seeing something that was to change the face and nature of the world. It was the opening of the Liverpool and Manchester Railway. Here, for the first time in history, was a railway between two important cities, with up and down roads and proper stations, even signalling of a very primitive sort, working all its goods and passenger traffic by steam power.

Railways of lesser sorts there were already, mostly connected with mining. Even the steam locomotive on rails had nearly a quarter of a century behind it. As for the vehicle on rails—the track-guided wagon—its history went back through the centuries. Charles E. Lee, in *The Evolution of Railways*, has traced the origins of prepared rutways, with uniform gauge, back to pre-Christian civilisations of the Eastern Mediterranean and Mesopotamia. The grooved road, with proper passing loops, was known to classic Greece, and its remains may still be seen in imperishable stone. Nameless engineers had discovered the value, for special heavy transport, of what might be called the disciplined way, the way that was smooth in rough places and which automatically guided its traffic.

Centuries went by. Empires were made, and crumbled. We can still see the ruts that guided the Roman wagons in the streets of Pompeii, and in many other places. Their average gauge, in modern measurement, was 1·445 metres, or just under 4 ft 9 in., which is the gauge of railways today in Western Europe including Great Britain, and throughout North America. A Roman specimen was discovered at Abbeydore in 1901, on the site of a Victorian railway station.

As far as we know, it was only with the end of the darker Middle Ages and the dawn of the Renaissance, that artificers conceived and put into practice the principle of the flanged wheel bearing on a raised rail, which not only guided but made very much smoother and easier the motion of a heavily laden vehicle, and was the

7

Richard Trevithick

essence of the true railway. As yet there was no demand for such a thing for nation-wide transport. Roads themselves, which the Romans understood so well, had become moribund. Travel was on horseback, or by litter. As for freight, the packhorse held his own on ways where a heavy wagon would get hopelessly bogged. But there were the mines, and it was in these that the first true railways appeared.

A mining truck on wooden rails was illustrated in a German treatise believed to have been published in 1519, but this shows a plain wheel with a flanged or grooved rail. The flanged wheel (or roller) on a plain rail was known, however, by the middle of the sixteenth century, notably in the German-worked gold-mines of Transylvania, and a specimen fortunately—and doubtless quite accidentally—was preserved for posterity. All parts were of wood, but it was a real railway, even having a primitive form of points with a single tongue.

During the succeeding centuries many mining railways were built, both on the Continent and in Great Britain. In Great Britain, indeed, they came much more out into the open, for they were built to carry coal from the pits down to the staithes or wharfs for barging and shipment by coastal craft. Still standing, and scheduled and preserved as an ancient monument, is the splendid Causey Arch on a branch of the Tanfield Wagon-Way in County Durham. It was built in 1727, and though already disused in the same century, it has lasted as the world's oldest railway bridge.

But the question of flanged rail or flanged wheel went on being argued, and both principles were applied until the early nineteenth century. Iron straps were laid on the once all-wooden rails, to bear flanged wheels. But then came a vogue for flanged iron plates to receive plain wheels. It was a flanged way that received the world's first steam railway locomotive, made and demonstrated by Richard Trevithick on the Penydarran mining tramroad, Merthyr Tydfil, in 1804.

It was Trevithick who had made the first high-pressure stationary engines, powerful and efficient for their day and far more compact than the enormous eighteenth-century low-pressure engines of James Watt and of Thomas Newcomen before him, which were as much structures as machines. The Trevithick engine made locomotion a practical proposition, first on the highway (1802) and then on rails, though in France Nicholas Cugnot, back in the seventeen-sixties, had made steam wagons which did in fact laboriously move themselves.

But the steam railway did not come with a rush. The earliest public lines used horse traction. There was the first public railway in the world, the Surrey Iron Railway from Wandsworth to Croydon, incorporated by an Act of May 21, 1801, and opened on July 26, 1803, some seven months before Trevithick's demonstration. On June 29, 1804, the world's first public passenger railway was incorporated, to be opened as the Oystermouth Railway between Swansea and the Mumbles on March 25, 1807. It lasted, latterly as an electric tramway, until 1960.

Trevithick's locomotive had a single horizontal cylinder embedded in its boiler, driving, through a cross-head on long projecting slidebars, a cranked shaft with an enormous flywheel.

Model of Murray/Blenkinsop locomotive, 1812, in the Science Museum, London

Power was transmitted to the axles through spur wheels. In short, it was Trevithick's stationary engine rigged up so that it would move along. Further, it could move a considerable load, and so placed itself above the status of a mere scientific model.

But it was not until 1812 that steam traction was put to real commercial use, and that was on the Middleton colliery railway, Leeds, itself dating back to 1758. By many it was thought that smooth wheel on smooth rail would slip too much. John Blenkinsop had therefore invented a rack rail, with which the locomotive engaged through a toothed driving wheel. Three engines were built by Matthew Murray during 1812–13, each with two vertical cylinders and transmission by gears. The system lasted until 1835, and the principle is still used for steep-grade mountain railways, such as the Mount Washington and Rigi lines.

The steam locomotive working by adhesion only, like Trevithick's, quickly had its champions. In 1813 William Hedley and Christopher Blackett produced *Puffing Billy* for the flanged plateway of Wylam Colliery, and on July 25, 1814, George Stephenson had his own first locomotive, subsequently named *Blucher*, in steam and in demonstration on the Killingworth colliery tramroad.

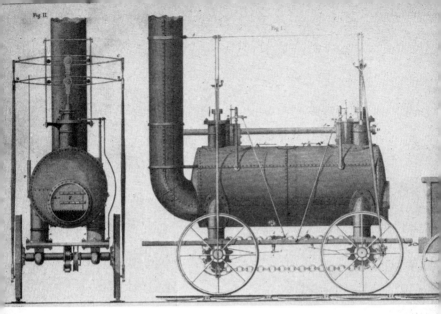

Stephenson locomotive with chain-coupled axles and steam springs, pre-1825

Stephenson was an engine-wright who had moved about the Tyne collieries (with a year's sojourn in Scotland, where he worked on a mill engine) all his life. He had been born beside the Wylam Colliery tramroad in 1781, and was 32 when he was given charge of the pit engine at Killingworth. Possibly an experimental and unsuccessful Trevithick locomotive in the North-East, and more probably Blackett's *Puffing Billy*, had inspired him to design and make something better. His first locomotive began with the name *My Lord*, for the proprietor at Killingworth, Lord Ravensworth, and acquired that of *Blucher* in a flush of enthusiasm for Prussian allies following the battle of Waterloo.

The Stephenson improvements were undoubted, but their effect was at first stultified by the wretched track of the period. Flanged plates for locomotive traction were hopeless, as *Puffing Billy's* sponsors quickly and ruefully discovered. Cast iron in any form was too fragile. Not until 1820, when a patent was granted to John Birkinshaw for rolled iron rails, which were produced at Bedlington, did the railway as we know it become possible, as an efficient and ultimately world-wide commercial machine. Steel rails came later in the century, progressively increasing in weight.

13

Stockton and Darlington opening, 1825,
from a drawing by J. R. Brown, believed to be contemporary

In the fifteen years that led from Stephenson's *Blucher* to his classic *Rocket*, quite a number of locomotives were built and worked for better or worse. There had been one or two ludicrous freaks. General design involved a centre-flue boiler, or one with a return flue, with vertical cylinders embedded in the top of it, and transmitting their power to the axles by transverse beams. There were four wheels, often unsprung. An ingenious arrangement, but one which did not persist, involved 'steam springs'—four cylindrical openings in the bottom of the boiler shell, each containing a piston supported by the axle below, so that the machine was hydraulically cushioned by its own boiler pressure. Trevithick had turned his exhaust into the chimney. Both Stephenson and his contemporary Timothy Hackworth refined that exhaust nozzle into a proper blast-pipe creating a constant draught.

On September 27, 1825, with the backing of the powerful Quaker family of the Peases, there was opened the first *public* railway to use locomotives, between Stockton and Darlington. The engines were to be by George Stephenson, beginning with the famous *Locomotion*, which is still in existence. According to its Act, the company was to work its traffic by 'men, horses or otherwise'. It was Stephenson who interpreted 'otherwise' to Edward Pease as meaning 'steam travelling engines'. Steam traction was successful, but for some time passengers were carried in horse-drawn coaches on flanged wheels, which dodged unassumingly between the heavy but slow steam coal trains. Timothy Hackworth did much of the subsequent locomotive work on the Stockton and Darlington Railway, and produced in *Royal George* (1827) the first engine with six coupled wheels.

Stephenson was aiming at fresh achievements. Almost entirely self-trained and self-educated (he was illiterate nearly to maturity), he had embraced the arts of the civil, as well as of the mechanical engineer, and when the much more imposing

George Stephenson

Liverpool and Manchester Railway was promoted by powerful Lancashire interests, it was he who was appointed Engineer. The splendour of his viaduct across the Sankey Valley, and his perseverance in building an embankment across the supposedly impassable bog of Chat Moss, made him famous. His success further swayed the directors in favour of locomotive haulage, whereas they had previously leaned towards stationary engines and cables.

They accordingly offered a £500 prize for a locomotive which should fulfil certain very strict conditions. With the prize would go certain purchase, and obviously a contract. Trials were to be held on the completed Rainhill Level of the Liverpool and Manchester Railway.

Now certain very important improvements were being made in locomotive design just before this. Stephenson had been joined by his son Robert, but there were rivals also. Marc Seguin in France was experimenting with steam traction down at St. Etienne, and, further, was making a multi-tubular (fire-tube) boiler, a very much more efficient steam generator than the old single-flue or return-flue boilers of the pioneers. He induced draught by rotary fans—a weak point of the design. John Ericsson from Sweden was giving attention to a light-weight engine. But the Stephensons themselves struck on the multi-tubular boiler, with the great benefit of exhaust-induced draught. Henry Booth, who came in as third partner for the Rainhill competition, probably had something to do with improved boiler design. Further, the old vertical cylinders in the top of the boiler, the clumsy (and hideous) arrangement of beam transmission and valve gear, were out. In 1828 the Stephensons had made an engine called *Lancashire Witch* for the Bolton and Leigh Railway. Though it perpetuated the old-style boiler, this time with two grates and flues, it had inclined outside cylinders at the footplate end. The same arrangement appeared on the Stephenson engine *Invicta*, built in the following year for the Canterbury and Whitstable Railway, and both these engines had their four wheels coupled. Early coupling of wheels had been by endless chains and sprockets, an arrangement both fragile and noisy. The coupling rod was the thing. It should be noted that the Canterbury and Whitstable Railway ante-dated the Liverpool and Manchester by nearly four months, from May 24, 1830. Not only, however, did it have a single track; most of it was worked by cable haulage with stationary engines. It was indeed the first steam public railway to carry passengers by such power, but did

Stephenson's *Rocket*, 1829 (replica made by Robert Stephenson and Co. for Henry Ford)

not qualify as the prototype of the locomotive-worked railway that was soon to come.

Up at Newcastle the classic *Rocket* was completed, and entered as suggested by the Stephensons and Henry Booth for the Rainhill Trials on the Liverpool and Manchester Railway. It had the multi-tubular boiler then being essayed by Seguin, fired at this stage by an external water-jacketed firebox believed to be by Booth. It had the inclined cylinders of the *Lancashire Witch* and the *Invicta*. Unlike its predecessors, it had single driving wheels, arranged 0–2–2. This engine's most famous challengers at Rainhill were Timothy Hackworth's *Sans Pareil*, with four coupled wheels, vertical cylinders at the sides, and a return-flue boiler, and the *Novelty*, which was entered by Captain Ericsson in partnership with John Braithwaite. Both were dogged by ill luck involving breakdowns. Considering the Swede's American success and fame in after years, one feels that he was unfortunate in his partnership. *Novelty's* weak point was an ingenious but scarcely practical boiler. A very light engine, she managed 30 miles an hour while she lasted, slightly in excess of the *Rocket's* top speed. There

Stephenson's *Northumbrian*, Liverpool and Manchester Railway, 1830
Contemporary drawing by Nasmyth

was no doubt about the *Rocket's* reliability; she fulfilled all the
conditions and completed this most famous of road tests without
the slightest hitch. The prize, and the Liverpool and Manchester
locomotive contract, went to the Stephensons.

The opening next year was scarcely auspicious. It was per-
formed by the Duke of Wellington, who was most unpopular in
Lancashire. The weather was vile. The Right Hon. William Huskis-
son was run down and killed by the *Rocket*. In the evening, with all
ceremony abandoned owing to the accident, there was the first
whiff of a new sort of crime. Somebody tried to derail the *Comet*,
which, however, was too strong for the wheelbarrow which had
been placed in her path.

For all this glum beginning, the railway was a tremendous success. Though prepared for the flow of inter-city passengers, the
directors were staggered by the flood of general merchandise. In
the Liverpool and Manchester line, the railway had arrived.

Edge Hill, Liverpool and Manchester Railway, about 1840

Pumping engines in the construction of Kilsby Tunnel, London and Birmingham Railway, 1837. Horse gin on upper right

One chooses the eighteen-sixties, rather than absolute mid-century, because that decade saw the first great mobile war, and also the first trans-continental railway from ocean to ocean, both in the United States. For in the meantime, transport revolution had crowned the Industrial Revolution.

North America had followed British pioneering very closely. On August 8, 1829, a locomotive called *Stourbridge Lion*, built in England by Foster, Rastrick and Company, had been steamed on a line built by the Delaware and Hudson Canal Company, but she broke up the track, and when this little railway was opened from Carbondale to Honesdale on October 9, it was worked by cables and gravity. The first American public railway, the Baltimore and Ohio, was opened with horse traction over a 13-mile stretch on May 24, 1830. A minute locomotive, *Tom Thumb*, by Peter Cooper, had indeed been given a trial in a rather rash race with a horse. The little engine got ahead, but owing to a breakdown the horse won. Phineas Davis soon after produced some grotesque, but workable steam locomotives, and one of them, on August 24, 1835, brought the first train into Washington.

Before this, the first section of the South Carolina Railroad was opened, on January 15, 1831, and this was the first regular steam public railway in the United States. Its original locomotive, the *Best Friend of Charleston*, did indeed explode, allegedly because the simple darkie fireman doctored the safety-valve in the interests of noise-abatement, but others followed, and the *Best Friend* herself was rebuilt, and appropriately renamed *Phoenix*. By 1833 the South Carolina Railroad extended from Charleston to Hamburg, which made it the longest railway in the world. Horatio Allen, who was responsible for its motive power, might well be cited as the George Stephenson of America.

These very early American locomotives were markedly different from the work of either the Stephensons or Timothy Hackworth. Those of Phineas Davis had vertical cylinders and boilers, while the *Best Friend*, although it had inclined inside cylinders, had an attenuated vertical boiler shaped like a hock bottle. Engines imported to the States from England followed British practice, and some built by Edward Bury, who had been too late for the Rainhill Trials, introduced to American practice the bar frame, which was to persist for as long as American steam did—considerably more than a century.

In England the *Rocket* type of locomotive did not last long, even with the improvement of an internal firebox. Stephenson's *Planet*, delivered to the Liverpool and Manchester Railway in October 1830, was a great advance. She had inside horizontal cylinders, under the smokebox, and the driving wheels at the rear. Elongation of the *Planet* type, with the addition of a trailing axle, produced Stephenson's *Patentee*, a basic prototype of engines which continued to be built until well on in the Victorian Era.

It could be built as a single driver, or with either the leading or trailing wheels, or both, coupled to the driving wheels in the middle. *Patentees* furnished the earliest motive power of several pioneer public railways in Continental Europe, including those of Belgium (Brussels–Mechlin, May 5, 1835), Germany (Nuremberg–Fürth, December 7, 1835), Russia (Pavlovsk–Tsarskoye Selo, October 9, 1836), the Netherlands (Amsterdam–Haarlem, September 24, 1839), and Italy (Naples–Portici, October 4, 1839.) It should be remarked that at that time neither Germany nor Italy were nations; the Nuremberg and Naples lines were respectively in Bavaria and the somewhat sinister Kingdom of the Two Sicilies.

Detail of Stephenson's *Adler* (Eagle) for the Nuremberg–Fürth Railway, 1835 (replica)

Neither aristocratic nor popular opinion was solidly behind the new railways; very much the opposite, in many cases. Their backers were the new, powerful, industrial and commercial classes, such as the Lancashire capitalists, who became known (and sometimes feared) as the Liverpool Party, and the rich Quaker families of the North-East. Fierce and often gory scrimmages took place between gangs of rough characters hired by both the landowners and the engineers who came to survey their land. There was tremendous rumpus over every fresh Railway Bill introduced into Parliament. Colonel Sibthorpe, the Hon. Member for Lincoln, greatly favoured shooting surveyors on sight, though he was never caught in such a prank. The Duke of Wellington was highly distrustful, although as Prime Minister he had consented to open the Liverpool and Manchester Railway. Rapid conveyance would enable the Fierce Unwashed to move about, with alarming possibilities of sedition and insurrection, both greatly feared at that time. This feeling, added to outrage at encroachment on land, was very general among the Tories, while the Whigs generally backed commercial interests, and were thus in favour.

South Yorkshire Railway, c. 1855; engine *Fitzwilliam*

London and Birmingham Railway bridge across the Grand Union Canal, with water-tower, near Blisworth; 1837

Away from England, attitudes varied. America received the train with joyous enthusiasm. It could and did open up vast areas of virgin and savage country to the enterprise of a young and vigorous nation. Consequently, in many American cities the train was to march proudly down the main streets, while in Great Britain the railway station would be kept as far as possible from the city centre and the 'best houses', as in Cambridge. Belgium, recently separated from the Netherlands proper, took a very progressive view. From the very beginning its railways were a State enterprise, designed for the most convenient service of the nation without wasteful duplication of routes through commercial competition. Far from producing a meagre railway system, this eventually resulted in Belgium having one of the busiest, and undoubtedly the densest railway networks in the world. But down in Italy the feudally fearsome King of the Two Sicilies had very different views. While he tolerated the little line round the Bay of Naples, the idea of long-distance connections was anathema. Who knew what revolutionary armies such lines might land on his doorstep overnight!

Once it was seen that a steam railway would work, and make a lot of money, industry and commerce became quickly more powerful at the expense of entrenched landowners. Railways began to spread rapidly. The first line in the Metropolis was the modest London and Greenwich Railway (1836), but in the following year there was the London and Birmingham Railway,

23

Mid-Victorian contrast: Francis Trevithick's London and North Western engine *Cornwall*, originally built in 1847 and now preserved at Clapham, alongside the Crewe Works tramway engine *Nipper*, from an engraving in *Engineering*

opened in stages from July 20, to be completed on September 17, 1838. As the Grand Junction Railway had been opened from Birmingham northwards, to join the Liverpool and Manchester, on July 4, 1837, the capital was thus connected to the great cities of the North-West as well as to the Midland industrial area. Robert Stephenson was Engineer of the London and Birmingham, with its great tunnel through the Kilsby Ridge. The easier Grand Junction was the work of Joseph Locke, who, however, also built the much more formidable London and Southampton, with its

splendid main line over the southern chalk. This was first opened as far as Woking on May 21, 1838, and throughout on May 11, 1840. It soon became the London and South Western Railway, as Portsmouth objected to the original title.

But slightly junior to the South Western, and in conception and construction the grandest railway yet built, was the Great Western, initially from London to Bristol, backed by the Merchant Venturers and, in London, by the wealthy firm of Gibbs and Company. Isambard Kingdom Brunel was its incomparable

Bury locomotive, London and Birmingham railway, 1837

Kilsby Tunnel; one of the great shafts

Travelling Post Office; restoration of the original Grand Junction carriage of 1838; *below* interior

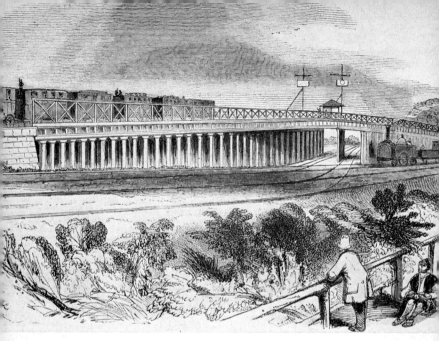

Norwood Flyover, London and Croydon Railway

Fox's Wood Tunnel, Great Western Railway, in 1841

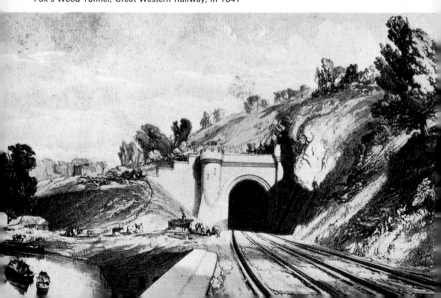

engineer, and he schemed his line on a scale which, with its original 7-ft gauge, might have set a standard for the world, if only it had been conceived earlier. Together with its later additions, it stands to this day as Brunel's monument, with such features as the almost imperceptible inclined plane rising from London to Swindon, the die-straight Box Tunnel through the Wiltshire oolite (both original) and the unique Royal Albert Bridge over the Tamar beyond Plymouth (Brunel's last great work, completed when he was dying in 1859). The broad gauge, alas, finally vanished in 1892. The first section of the G.W.R. was opened as far as Taplow on June 4, 1838. It was completed to Bristol on June 30, 1841.

Before that, many minor lines and several major ones had opened elsewhere. The Leeds and Selby dated back to 1834, as did the first Irish railway from Dublin to Kingstown. The Newcastle and Carlisle was complete by May 21, 1839. The Birmingham and Gloucester, the Midland Counties, the North Midland and the York and North Midland were all done by the summer of 1840, bringing York on to the national system. It was to become a supremely important railway centre. Expansion was now steady, in a business-like way, and to regulate traffic between different

I. K. Brunel's station at Temple Meads, Bristol

J. U. Rastrick's Ouse Valley Viaduct near Hayward's Heath on the Brighton main line; opened for traffic in 1841

railways the Railway Clearing House was established at the beginning of 1842. While isolated railways had appeared in Scotland, we should note particularly the Edinburgh and Glasgow Railway (February 21, 1842).

Robert Stephenson's 'long-boiler' type of the eighteen-forties: *Lord Robartes*

Old Euston : the Propylaeum

York was mentioned just now. In that city was a draper, one George Hudson. In many ways he was a most unpleasant character, but he foresaw the enormous expansion that was coming. He also knew the value of amalgamating small undertakings

Milford Tunnel, North Midland Railway, in the eighteen-forties

Thomas Brassey, greatest of the early Victorian railway contractors

Kitching's *Derwent*, a Hackworth type locomotive, Stockton and Darlington Railway, 1845; in steam at Darlington in 1925

Railway and waterway in the eighteen-forties; Manchester and Leeds Railway

into big companies. His business methods were deplorable (jiggery-pokery with the York and North Midland led to his eventual undoing), but while he rode the terrific wave of railway speculation in the middle-forties, he became the originator of much of our most important railway mileage. During 1845 public interest in railway schemes rapidly increased, and in the following year the investors went railway-mad. While 272 Acts were passed for new railways, there were innumerable schemes (some utterly preposterous) in which money, itself often imaginary, was sunk and lost. It was a great scandal, and earned the industry a bad name, which was wholly undeserved by the railway as a transport machine.

Through the 'fifties the expansion continued, as it did also in North America and other areas, but it must be said that in the English-speaking countries it was worse planned than in many others. In Great Britain, and even more in the United States, it was a commercial rat-race caused by an almost mystic reverence for private enterprise. Belgium, as we have seen, started with State railways. Prussia proceeded in a direction which, at its best,

Midnight passport inspection, from Doyle's drawing in a Victorian *Punch*

Robert Stephenson's tubular Britannia Bridge across the Menai Straits, 1850

had an eye to national welfare, and at its worst, was militaristic; the same was true of the then Austrian Empire and of Russia. The King of Hanover, however, made all trains terminate in his capital with no connections. People kept waiting for hours were expected to go shopping. France divided her country regionally and granted concessions to companies, each to have an area monopoly.

In the sparsely populated British colonies the Continental line had fortunately to be taken. The first British colonial railways were the Champlain and St Lawrence in Canada, 1836; and in the later Crown Colonies the Jamaica Railway (1845). It seems quaint that the Demarara Railway (opened 1848) in British Guiana was senior by six years to the first Australian steam railway (Melbourne to Port Melbourne, September 12, 1854).

Mechanical advances should be noted here. The earliest visual signalling was by hand, flag, or lamp, and the signalmen were sworn policemen. For many years, semaphores had been used for overland telegraphy, both by Government and under companies, such as Watsons. In 1841 they were first used (at New Cross, London) for the control of train movements. But in the same year Cooke and Wheatstone's electric telegraph was used in conjunction with a 'block system' (no two trains in one section at one time) to control movements through Clay Cross Tunnel on the North Midland Railway. By degrees, disgracefully slow for the most part and stimulated only by periodic accidents, a combination of block telegraph and semaphores became general, and

Seal of the Wigan Branch Railway

35

The Jenny Lind type. It originated at Leeds Railway Foundry in 1847. This was London, Brighton and South Coast No. 122, built in 1856

ultimately compulsory on British railways. Charles H. Gregory, who had adapted the semaphore to railway use, used a system of partial interlocking (points and signals) in 1843, but complete interlocking did not appear until it was patented by John Saxby in 1856. In railway signalling, as in motive power, Great Britain gave the world its guiding light. In fairness we should mention the independent work on interlocking by Vignier on the Western Railway of France (1855).

Locomotive advances were chiefly in size and power, but the use of steam expansively in the cylinders, by variation in the position of the valve gear, was a notable advance of the 'forties. Such a thing had been devised by Sir Goldsworthy Gurney, a gifted designer of steam road coaches, but its application on railway locomotives came in the early 'forties, classic pioneers being Alexander Allan, the brothers Daniel and John Gooch, and Robert Stephenson and Company, all of whom produced reliable forms of link motion, which were to continue being made into the present century, when radial valve gears became general in modern practice.

At this same time Daniel Gooch on the Great Western was building the largest, fastest, and most powerful locomotives in the world. It must be noted that American engines, then and for some time to come, remained very small and light. The tracks on which they ran were often of the most flimsy sort. But that also led to the early use in the States of bogies or pivoted trucks, both for loco-motives and for vehicles. In the former case original honours may

36

be divided between John B. Jervis (U.S.A.) and Robert Stephenson and Company, but the arrangement was distrusted by British companies. The world owes bogie vehicles to America, and to Ross Winans in particular, though in England both Joseph Wright and W. Bridges Adams tried to persuade obdurate managements. Gooch's splendid express engines on the broad-gauge Great Western were entirely rigid eight-wheelers, and on such a road there was no trouble at all. In 1848 the best express down from Paddington to the West averaged 57 m.p.h. on the first $52\frac{1}{2}$ miles to Didcot. On a test run on May 11 of that year, with a train including Gooch's dynamometer car, the engine *Great Britain* averaged just under 67 m.p.h. over the same stretch, a world record without approach for many years.

British and Continental carriages were indeed very light, and apart from first-class coaches were usually a reproach to their owners. Their American and Russian counterparts, though often much larger, were often gaunt and comfortless. Freight vehicles

Daniel Gooch, in 1845, aged 29; the father of express trains

Joseph Beattie's *Windsor* (South Western, 1852). Note headgear of enginemen and policeman!

long continued to be of the crudest sort. Until improvements in rolling stock later in the century had a corresponding effect on the weight of trains, most locomotives were very small by British and Central European standards. Thomas Russell Crampton's patent engines with a long, rigid wheelbase and very large driving wheels right at the back, built during the 'forties and 'fifties, were fast

Queen Victoria, Louis Philippe, and Prince Albert on the London and South Western Railway, 1844

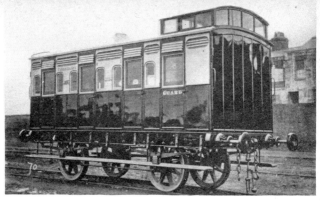

A mid-Victorian third-class carriage—this was a South Eastern specimen—was usually nightmarish

runners provided the loads were light. They enjoyed a considerable vogue in France and the German States. William Bridges Adams built very light locomotives, for running with but one or two coaches on lines of limited traffic. Pressures were generally very low by later standards; on most lines anything in excess of 50 lb. per square inch was considered rash to the point of recklessness.

Freaks abounded in old America! Stevens' 'Crampton' on the Camden and Amboy Railroad

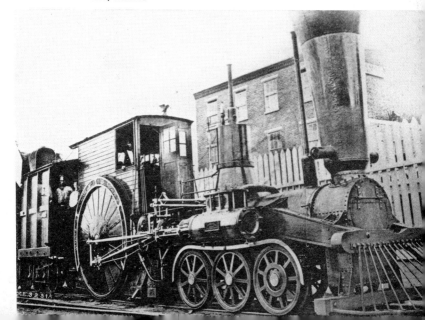

Swedish troop train (Halmstad–Nässjö Railway) in 18/8. Engine by Fox Walker, Bristol

I. K. Brunel's last great work: Royal Albert Bridge, Plymouth–Saltash (1859)

Relic of the Second Empire: Crampton patent locomotive *Le Continent*, built for the Paris–Strasbourg Railway in 1852 and still workable

Apart from the largest broad-gauge engines on the Great Western, the 'big engines' of the mid-nineteenth century were to be found in the Pennsylvania coalfields and in Austria on the Semmering Railway, the first line across the Alps (opened July 17, 1854). In such localities eight-coupled wheels were already being employed at a very early stage.

Long distances called for early improvements in carriage design in the United States and in Russia. Lavatories (rather a courtesy title at first) were installed, and there were many and sometimes quite fantastic attempts to produce satisfactory sleeping cars. George M. Pullman successfully converted three Chicago and Alton day coaches into sleepers during 1858–59, and in 1865 produced his classic *Pioneer*, the first true Pullman sleeping car, with convertible seats below and folding berths above.

Between the two events, America had her Civil War between the Northern and Southern States. Opening on traditional lines, it went well at first with the Confederates in the South, but superior Northern industrial resources and, above all, transport, turned the tide. Troops rushed up in convoys of trains could change the

42

Queen Victoria's day and night saloons, London and North Western Railway, 1869

The Prodigy of 1870. Patrick Stirling's No. 1, Great Northern Railway. Now at York Museum, she last steamed in 1938

Ancient lamp trolley at London Victoria. The 'pots' in the upper rack were dropped through holes in the carriage roofs

J. I. Cudworth's South Eastern Mail Engine, 1861

outcome of battle and often did so. Sherman's Georgia campaign depended, up to the capture of Atlanta, on the railway connections in his rear and the lines of the Louisville and Nashville and Western and Atlantic Railroads, which he captured as he advanced. United States Military Railroads formed two commands, East and West. To the North went the first victory in history to be won on mechanical locomotion.

By this time, railways were widespread in many parts of the world, but mostly in Europe and North America. By 1863, when the Inverness and Perth Junction Railway was completed, the British railway system extended from West Cornwall to the Moray Firth, and was still growing. The West Coast Route to Scotland had been completed in 1848 by the opening of the Caledonian Railway on February 15, the Lancaster and Carlisle Railway having been finished in the previous year. By August 1, 1848, there was an unbroken route from London (Euston) to Aberdeen via Carlisle, Carstairs, and Perth. The bridging of the Tyne and Tweed water-gaps in 1850 virtually completed the East Coast Route as far as Edinburgh. The first East Coast express left London (Maiden Lane) on August 5, though King's Cross, the new and splendid terminus of the Great Northern, was not opened until 1852. A much shorter, but very significant British opening was that of the first section of the underground Metropolitan Railway from Bishops Road, Paddington, to Farringdon Street in Central London, on January 10, 1863. Steam locomotives were used, with surface condensers to take care of the exhaust.

Northern Gothic: Gothenburg old station, Swedish State Railways, about 1860

In Continental Europe many of the main lines had been built north of the Balkans, but the great Alpine tunnels were not yet built, and the mountains still formed a vast barrier extending from the Semmering in the east to the Rhône valley in the west.

In America the great—the tremendous—event was the building of the mighty trans-continental line from the Missouri to the Pacific Coast. The Union Pacific company pushed west; the Central Pacific pushed east from California, shipping its equipment round Cape Horn and facing the great rampart of the high Sierras. In 1869 the two advancing parties met in Utah, and on May 10

Meeting of the Union Pacific and Central Pacific Railroads, May 10, 1869. CPRR *Jupiter* (left) and UPRR No. 119

Riggenbach's first rack line, Kahlenberg, Austria, 1866

Riggenbach's Vitznau–Rigi Railway, 1871–73

On the Central Pacific Railroad, 1869

London and North Western guard, *c.* 1850

Pride and pomp: Windows in the North Stafford Hotel, Stoke

Victorian Panorama: Dover Priory, London, Chatham and Dover Railway, *c.* 1865

Mid-Victorian lark: 'Yesterday, one of the Caledonian Company's engines exploded, so we all had our pictures taken . . .'

the Central Pacific engine *Jupiter* and Union Pacific No. 119 moved slowly forward and touched pilots at Promontory Point. Freight could be sent, and passengers carried, from the Atlantic Coast to the Pacific by railroad.

America by this time showed a strange mixture of the primitive and the advanced. Nearly all her railway mileage was single track, worked by a sadly fallible train-order system, and the permanent way was sometimes of the rockiest sort. Locomotives were largely of the light four-coupled sort, with outside cylinders and leading bogies. Except in the Eastern States, wood was the usual fuel. The best trains, while they loafed across state and continent to the clangour of their brass engine bells, included sumptuous Pullman cars. They seemed faultless apart from a distressing liability to catch fire if they hit each other or anything upset them.

Already, a century ago, the railway was seen as a machine that had conquered the old world and was making a new one. That indeed is what it did. The motor and the aircraft followed in its wake, but the locomotive was the conqueror of land distances.

Burning of the Irish Mail at
Abergele, August 20, 1868

The third-class revolution,
1875. The Midland company
scandalised its neighbours
by stuffing *all* the carriage
seats
*Photomontage by author.
Mock-up by British Rail-
ways Historical Relics, Clapham*

By 1876 the British railway system was almost complete, for that year saw the opening of the Midland Railway north of Settle to Carlisle, making a third main line between English and Scottish cities. Two years before, in the far north, the rails had reached Wick and Thurso, where they still terminate. Of important lines there remained to be built the Great Central (last line into London, via Nottingham, Leicester, and Aylesbury, 1899) and the West Highland (to Fort William in 1894 and on to Mallaig in the late 'nineties, though opening was not until 1901). There were already two much older lines to the West Highland coast, the Callander and Oban, and the Dingwall and Skye.

Very important was the closing of the Scottish water-gaps of Forth and Tay, which had seen the world's first train ferries (1850 and 1851). The first Tay Bridge was opened in 1878, but fell with a train at the end of 1879, a national calamity. Its very substantial, if ugly, successor, was over two miles long and was opened in 1887. The superb Forth Bridge of John Fowler and Benjamin Baker, still one of the largest bridges in the world, with two main cantilever spans of 1,710 ft each, followed in 1890. These at last completed the East Coast Route from London to Dundee and Aberdeen. The year 1895 saw the famous 'races' from London to Aberdeen over the rival routes, when, albeit with very lightly loaded trains, there was some extraordinarily fast running on both lines. On the West Coast and on the same night, the London and North Western engine *Hardwicke* and the Caledonian engine No. 17 both averaged 67·2 m.p.h. start-to-stop, from Crewe to Carlisle and from Perth to Aberdeen respectively. A happy time was had by all except the unlucky passengers, who found themselves unloaded on a sleeping city with several hours to breakfast-time. Another water-gap, down in England, was the Severn Estuary. After enormous difficulties, the Severn Tunnel was opened in 1886, four miles between the Gloucestershire and Monmouthshire portals, the longest under-water tunnel in the world.

In North America other trans-continental lines, such as the Northern Pacific and the Santa Fe–Southern Pacific routes, followed the original one through Utah, but the most romantic

53

'Midland'. Sir James Allport's wily benevolence

Cable-assisted train on Cowlairs incline, Glasgow, *c.* 1895

'North Western'. Sir Richard Moon's sneer of cold command

Lancashire and Yorkshire locomotive, built by the London and North Western Railway in 1873

Fall of the first Tay Bridge in the great storm of December 28, 1879

Forth Bridge : Inchgarvie Piers

The Forth Bridge, by Fowler and Baker, shortly before opening in 1890

adventure of this sort was the building of the Canadian Pacific Railway, considerably backed by the Hudson's Bay Company. Part of the motive was certainly political, to foil the secession or American annexation of British Columbia. It was a tremendous work, with the most formidable crossing of the Rockies yet made. The first through train rumbled from Montreal to Port Moody, B.C., June 28–July 4, 1886, taking 139 hours. The line reached Vancouver in the following year.

Quadrupling of track in the boom years sometimes produced parallel viaducts, as at Wilmslow, Cheshire

Euston-Liverpool express in the 'nineties: Ramsbottom *Problem* piloting Webb *Teutonic*

Great Western local, *c.* 1892, approaching Bath. Observe mixed gauge

'John Hick' class three-cylinder compound engine, London and North-Western Railway. Early 'nineties

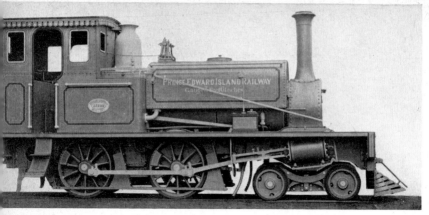

Canadian rarity : 3 ft 6 in. gauge Hunslet tank engine for the Prince Edward Island Railway, 1872

Currier and Ives print *American Express Train*. Time is in the eighteen-sixties. Admirably accurate, such prints became an American classic

Victorian English engines in Europe. This wood-burning 0–4–4 tank engine was built by Yorkshire Engine Company for the Poti–Tiflis Railway in 1879

Untidy design distinguished many Continental locomotives of the late nineteenth century; for example, Krauss and Company's *Stettin*, built in 1889 and here shown at Munich Central

Architectural pride; Kingsbridge, Dublin

In Continental Europe the first of the great Alpine Tunnels was built. Oldest was the inaccurately named Mont Cenis (under the Col de Frejus) between Italy and France. Over the pass proper, a three-rail line on J. B. Fell's system for steep grades (engine gripping the central rail) had been laid largely on Napoleon's old road and worked from 1868, but thanks to the successful

Cologne in the 'nineties

application of power drilling, the tunnel was completed by 1871, providing a direct route from Western Europe to Turin and all the Italian peninsula beyond. It was $8\frac{1}{2}$ miles long and was of course worked by steam, giving a smoky but entirely workable passage. The St. Gotthard Tunnel, which was also worked by steam until 1921 and was 9 miles 562 yards long, followed in 1882, giving a direct route from Germany to Milan, under the Lepontine Alps. Before this, in 1884, Austria had built the Arlberg Tunnel, nearly $6\frac{1}{2}$ miles long, east to west through the mountains between the Tyrol and Vorarlberg.

During this time regular, as opposed to occasional, use of the rail for travel had led to great improvements in carriage design. Pullman's sleeping cars, as noted, began in the 'sixties. The Belgian Georges Nagelmackers' sleepers, with separate cabins,

Late Victorian sumptuosities: Family saloon for the Manchester, Sheffield and Lincolnshire Railway, built in 1891; Midland Railway dining carriage furnished 'regardless' by Waring and Gillow, 1896

began in the 'seventies. The North Eastern Railway built single-berth sleeping compartments in 1894, and was soon imitated. Dining cars appeared, and so did the European side-corridor train. These things led to greatly increased weight, with a corresponding rise in the size and dimensions of locomotives. Steam pressures went up, and so did the capacity of boilers relative to the capacity of cylinders. John F. McIntosh of the Caledonian Railway was a famous British exponent of this improved ratio, beginning with the Dunalastair class express engines of 1896. At the same time fuel economy was sought through compound expansion, and was most successfully applied by de Glehn and du Bousquet in France. It was used extensively, but with limited success, by Francis Webb and Thomas Worsdell in England, where W. M. Smith produced what were ultimately better results, in an experimental engine on the North Eastern Railway, which lasted very many years. Superheating, which involved the splitting-up of the live-steam passage into a great number of small tubes, and their exposure in special large flue-tubes to the hot firebox gases, was first successfully applied by Schmidt in 1898, on two Prussian State express locomotives (4—4—0, class P4). It took about a

The first British ten-wheeler (Highland No. 103, 1894) heads the last steam train from Inverness. Forres 1965

Giant's Causeway line ; the first in the world to use electric traction generated by water power (1883)

Veta Pass, Denver and Rio Grande Railroad in the 'eighties

decade for the arrangement to be fully accepted, which was the way of great mechanical improvements at that time. Steam pressures in ordinary practice went up to 140 lb. per square inch and on to 180 lb., or even higher in exceptional cases; Dugald Drummond tried 200 lb. on the Caledonian in 1889. Pressures tended to be higher with compound locomotives, and sometimes lower when superheating was employed. The largest steam locomotives, then and henceforward, were to be found in North America.

The motor-car, or the internal-combustion engine in any form, was as yet a curiosity, but as far back as 1879 at an exhibition in Berlin people had been conveyed on a very small electric train, whose locomotive (on which the motorman sat astride!) was the work of Werner Siemens. German experiments with electric trams followed, and on August 3, 1883, the first trip was made

King William Street; the now vanished terminus of the world's first electric underground railway, the City and South London, 1890

First main-line electrification; Camden–Waverly Tunnel, Baltimore and Ohio Railroad, 1895
Locomotive by Westinghouse

on Magnus Volk's still surviving electric railway along Brighton beach, the first example in England. On September 28 Ireland saw the first use of electric traction with hydro-electric power on the little Giant's Causeway line from Portrush. On December 18, 1890, the first electric underground railway, the City and South London, was opened between Central London and what were then the southern suburbs. This was the world's first electric 'tube', though a briefly extant cable line, the Tower Subway, had been opened as far back as August 1870. The first electric haulage of main-line trains followed in August 1895, on the Baltimore tunnel section of the Baltimore and Ohio Railroad in the United States.

Though local goods and passenger services for long remained quite incredibly slow on most lines, the average speeds of the fastest passenger trains in certain countries, notably Great Britain, France, and the United States, were, by now, often in excess of 50 m.p.h., with maximum speeds in the region of 75 m.p.h.

Mid-Victorian smash. The 10.0 pm Waterloo to Hampton Court theatre train in collision at Nine Elms; September 11, 1880. Seven killed

Many mechanical and electrical safeguards, which, formerly, had been regarded as academically interesting, became essential, and indeed were compelled upon railways by law. Such, in Great Britain, was the block system of signalling, with various forms of token or staff-and-ticket systems on single-track lines, which made it, at least theoretically, impossible for two trains in opposing directions to occupy the same section. With a lower frequency of services, American railroads continued to work trains over such lines by telegraph and train-order, with a greater likelihood of human failure. Though real trouble was about equally terrible, whatever the system that had been abused, accidents were then much more frequent on American lines. In busy areas, however, America had introduced electric track circuits, giving the positions of trains to signalmen, as far back as the '70s.

Then, too, the necessity of continuous power brakes had been fully recognised, but the position was bedevilled by claims for rival systems—compressed air, vacuum, hydraulic or mechanical, automatic or non-automatic in action—as well as the reluctance of some companies to spend too much on very expensive equipment. Undoubtedly the best yet was the American automatic air brake of George Westinghouse. Non-automatic brakes were most pernicious things; S. Y. Smith's vacuum brake, for example, which became inoperative on vehicles detached from their locomotive. Several bad accidents with this brake culminated in one on the Great Northern Railway (Ireland) near Armagh in 1889 so frightful that the Government at last made rapid moves.

Henceforth, passenger trains had to be equipped with automatic power brakes, but the law did not insist on any one system being made a national standard. Companies made their own choice between Westinghouse automatic air brakes and automatic vacuum brakes. In the case of both, fracture of connections led to immediate brake application. But the absurdity of the position—doubtless dictated by the Anglo-Saxon horror of monopoly—can be exemplified by some specimen through journeys. From London, King's Cross, to Inverness, there were vacuum brakes with Great Northern haulage as far as York; then Westinghouse air over the North Eastern and North British to Perth. North of Perth the Highland Railway took the through carriages on vacuum. From London to Edinburgh via Leeds it was vacuum as far as Carlisle (Midland Railway) and air thereafter on the North British. Consequently, through-running vehicles had to be dual-fitted. Of the five big companies working south of the Thames–Severn line, the London, Chatham and Dover used Westinghouse air, the South Eastern used vacuum, the London, Brighton and South Coast used air, while the South Western and the Great Western used vacuum again. Locomotives working into 'foreign territory' had to be dual-fitted like the coaches. North America, France, and Germany wisely went for air brakes on their main lines. Various vacuum brakes turned up in northern and south-eastern Europe—and so it was about the world. Air was used for electric trains, even though they ran on lines which used vacuum for steam trains. There had been a Battle of the Brakes, just as there had been a Battle of the Gauges, but the former was never properly resolved—a monument to British Governmental, rather than mechanical, stupidity. But Government, more especially that in English-speaking countries, has always been particularly dim when it comes to transport policy!

Twentieth century

This is an arbitrary sub-title, for a certain railway phase really belonged to the last decade of the nineteenth century and the first of the twentieth. That phase was distinguished in several countries by high flights in the way of maximum speed. Where railways were concerned, it must be admitted that the great examples of speeding came chiefly from those countries where rival railway companies were in close competition for the same traffic between the same cities, and that meant Great Britain and the United States. The only really high speeds in regular service, where railway authorities had territorial monopoly, were in France, whose Northern Railway had some of the most lively express services in the world, while the Midi Railway people rushed their trains from Bordeaux to Dax simply because they were sporting Frenchmen and the straight, level road *asked for it*.

London, Chatham and Dover Continental express near Bickley in the eighteen-nineties

West Coast sleeping berth, 1906
Author's photomontage

American-built Pullman, Brighton line, 1906

New York Central locomotives by William Buchanan (eighteen-nineties) still in local service about 1930

Eastern Railway of France local in the 'nineties. The leading engine, *Odessa*, is a Crampton patent dating from the 'fifties

Old enemies in the United States were the New York Central and the Pennsylvania companies, running rival services between New York and Chicago, and both having much better tracks than were then common in North America. U.S. 'records' had long been more numerous than authentic; possibly the first claim to 'one hundred miles an hour' had been made by some Northern engineer who had successfully driven through a Confederate ambush in the 'sixties. But on May 10, 1893, William Buchanan's superb engine, New York Central No. 999, on a very fast run with the Empire State Express from New York to Buffalo, was clocked over a measured stretch at 112·5 m.p.h. near Grimesville. The engine was a very large version of what was the traditional American 4–4–0 type, and fortunately has been preserved. British commentators, used to American claims, have long been cautious, but this one has never been disproved. It was a world land-speed record for many years.

Northern Railway of France express in the 'nineties. 'Outrance' class engine

Early in the present century, there was intense competition between the Great Western and the South Western companies for American traffic between Plymouth and London. The London and South Western route was shorter but more arduous. On May 9, 1904, Charles Rous-Marten timed the up Ocean Mail of the Great Western, with the engine *City of Truro* attaining a maximum speed of 102 m.p.h. down Wellington Bank. On July 1, 1906, the South Western's boat train was derailed at high speed, with heavy loss of life, at Salisbury. On the same day the Great Western completed a cut-off, making a shorter route to the West. Since then there has been no more racing between rival British railways. *City of Truro*, like the American engine, is preserved.

Tyneside commuters in 1904

In the same decade, heavy electric traction was engaging attention. Germany was not a country of high speeds (though its punctuality was exemplary), but it was there that the most spectacular records were set up. On a specially prepared stretch of military railway between Marienfelde and Zossen, two electric motor coaches each attained a maximum of 130 m.p.h. in 1903. This record was to remain unbroken until 1931.

Had people known, railway transport was now at its zenith. The motor, though advancing, was a preserve of the rich. Aircraft, though they certainly arrived, remained part-academic and part-sporting. The rail maintained a virtual monopoly of heavy land transport; further, certain British railways, such as the North

79

Great Central guard, *c.* 1905

On Field Hill, British Columbia, *c.* 1935

Eastern and the South Western, were very considerable owners of docks, and many of the major British companies owned ships plying in the narrow seas. Southampton owed all of its renaissance to the London and South Western Railway, having been quite a minor port until that company took over its docks in the eighteen-nineties.

Attempts had been made at a very early stage to provide some

form of visible or audible warning in the cabs of locomotives, to supplement the fixed signals, especially in foggy or other bad weather. There were two factors against such improvements, apart from the defects of early experimental apparatus. One was their expense; the other was the theory that elaborate mechanical aids made operating staff less alert and self-reliant. If the machine broke down, probably the man would do the same. Certainly, a

The manual locking frame. The old box at Liverpool Street, London; three signal-men, 165 levers

very bad collision in Clayton Tunnel on the Brighton line in 1861 originated with the failure of a primitive automatic signal and the ensuing fluster of a poor wretch who made an ambiguous inquiry on the old single-needle telegraph and then put out a white flag when it should have been red. But more often than not, this attitude by the railways was rather a specious excuse. Government inspecting officers made recommendations that were sometimes wise and sometimes foolish, but either way, the companies were not obliged to abide by the recommendations, and frequently ignored them.

On January 1, 1906, the Great Western Railway introduced audible cab signalling experimentally on the Henley branch. Later, this was developed into what was called 'automatic train control', actuated by ramps between the rails at all distant signals on Great Western main lines. Serious accidents became very rare on the G.W.R.

English Southern upper-quadrant semaphore, 1950

Heyday of the semaphore; gantry with stop and shunt signals for up and down roads at St. Pancras, Midland Railway, about fifty years ago

Characteristic lower-quadrant semaphores; Midland Railway signals with track-circuit indicators on the posts

Steam underground; Metropolitan No. 48 on a Hammersmith—New Cross train, just before electrification in 1905

Last steam mountain railway in Switzerland; Brienz-Rothorn

Descending to the Rhône Valley; Berne–Lötschberg–Simplon Railway ▶

Semaphores remained the usual form of fixed signals throughout the world's railways, though they differed greatly in appearance from country to country, working in the upper quadrant in such countries as the German States, or in the lower quadrant in the British Isles, Italy, and the Americas, to take but a few examples. British lines went over to upper quadrant from the 'thirties onwards, except on the Great Western Railway. Automatic semaphores, which went to danger immediately each train passed them at 'clear', made their appearance early in the century on the London and South Western Railway and on the North Eastern. Manual operation was succeeded by power (pneumatic or electric) in certain places. Automatic colour-light signals came into increasing use after 1920, at first on electric city railways.

These last had greatly increased since the début of the little City and South London in 1890. There was the nucleus of the present London tube system. The District and Metropolitan lines were electrified in 1905, two years after the Mersey Railway in Liverpool, where indeed the now vanished Liverpool Overhead Railway dated back to 1893. It was the world's first electric 'elevated'. Later, Germany and France both copied, to some extent, and in New York, where there were much older railways built over streets, these were electrified under pressure of law, which in the interests of what would now be called a 'smokeless zone' enforced electric traction on all railways entering Manhattan.

Long-distance electric traction was still in its infancy, but railway companies with heavy suburban traffic found themselves obliged to electrify suburban lines to compete with the electric tramways which were now invading the roads, and which lifted their user by the million. Before 1914 the North Eastern, Lancashire and Yorkshire, and the London, Brighton and South Coast had already done so. In the United States there was a boom in the now vanished 'inter-urban' electric line.

These last were ultimately to die by the hand of the motor. Their life has been more extended in parts of Germany (the very lively Cologne–Bonn Railway, for example) and in the Low Countries. But electrified suburban lines of main-line railways were destined for an immense, and apparently permanent, future. Tube lines, too, were extended to outlying suburbs.

Northern portal of the Simplon (second tunnel, 1921). The nature of the freight is obvious

Long-distance electric traction made its first strides in countries poor in coal but rich in water-power. In Europe a start was made with the Burgdorf–Thun line in Switzerland (1899), and in 1903 on the Valtellina line in Northern Italy, both using a three-phase system with alternating current at 750 and 3,000 volts respectively. It was the earliest beginning of the now vast Alpine electrification. This was furthered by the building of two new long Alpine tunnels. The first of the Simplon tunnels between Switzerland and Italy, 12 miles and 537 yards long, was completed and opened on June 1, 1906. It saw what might have been called token passages under steam, but virtually from the beginning this, the longest unbroken railway tunnel in the world, was electrically worked. It was originally a three-phase line, but was converted to the present Swiss 15,000-volt single-phase system, with a

The first British *Pacific*; G. J. Churchward's unique engine *The Great Bear*, built for the Great Western in 1908

Pullman to Edinburgh;
Queen of Scots leaving King's Cross, 1925

frequency of 16⅔ cycles, in 1930. The Berne–Lötschberg–Simplon
Railway (French capital) with its 9 miles, 140 yards tunnel, link-
ing the Simplon route with the railway system of Central Europe,
was opened in 1913, on the single-phase system from the start,
though the frequency was later raised from 15 to 16⅔ cycles.

   To many, now, there came a vision of the electrical revolution;

but to most people it flashed and rumbled but distantly, like a remote Alpine thunderstorm. In the meantime, steam was very much
alive, as indeed it was to remain until mid-century. Steam locomotives were already becoming very large engines, particularly in
North America, where public insistence on heavy car construction
for protection in wrecks, and public fancy for extravagant luxury

93

Standard and narrow gauge; Waterhouses in the Manifold
Valley, North Staffordshire, *c.* 1933

Neat inadequacy; Bergslagen Railways No. 46, built in 1900, being flogged along with a Falun—Gothenburg express

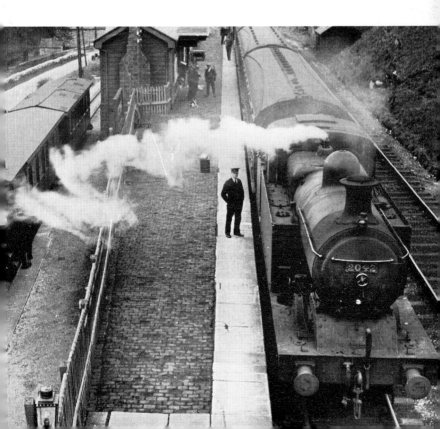

at substantial prices, resulted in a twelve-car train taring as much as a thousand tons. In Europe vehicles remained lighter, though not necessarily at the expense of comfort and convenience. Still the massive steel corridor coaches of Germany—the admirable *D-Wagen*—were beginning to set a general European standard. In both France and Germany the mighty Pacific-type (4–6–2) express engine had made its début before 1910, and there was one solitary example—Churchward's *The Great Bear* of 1908—on the Great Western Railway in England. Outstanding express locomotives of this time were the four-cylinder simple 4–6–0 'Star' class, also by Churchward on the Great Western, the French compounds, four-and six-coupled by de Glehn and du Bousquet in France, and the four-cylinder compound Pacifics built by Maffei in South Germany. Eight-coupled steam locomotives were general for heavy mineral and freight traffic over much of Europe. Semi-articulated engines after the style of Anatole Mallet, with two sets of driving wheels and cylinders under a single enormous boiler, were becoming general for coal haulage in the United States. Superheating, in several varieties but always following Schmidt's smoke-tube scheme, advanced gradually, and then more rapidly. Radial valve gears, initiated by Egide Walschaert in Belgium during the previous century, began to supersede the link motions of Gooch, Allan and Stephenson.

First Trans-Australian train leaving Kalgoorlie, October 15, 1917

War and peace

Had people known it in that blazing August of 1914, the tremendous and terrible war which broke out so suddenly was to run like a geological fault through history, mechanical history included. Over four years later British railwaymen could look back with some pride. One of the most brilliant movements immediately followed the outbreak of war when, chiefly over the London and South Western Railway, the British Expeditionary Force was landed without hitch in France in the space of sixteen days. It involved 689 special trains carrying 126,496 men with all their weapons, equipment, horses and vehicles, and about 5,000 tons of stores. Throughout the war traffic was immensely heavy, without corresponding maintenance. Only one British line came near breakdown, the struggling Highland Railway, far from rich, and mostly single-track, now forming the main supply line to the Fleet at Scapa and Invergordon. The situation was saved by a sort of mechanical transfusion of some twenty locomotives from other railways. German railways were adequate and well found; French lines less so, and the British Army's Railway Operating Division mustered many hundreds of locomotives. The attenuated and relatively obsolete Russian railways broke down, leading to defeat and revolution in the East.

For our present purposes this war stressed not only the importance of adequate transport in military success; it involved also the rapid, regardless-of-cost development of new locomotional means. Motor transport, aided by post-war disposal of surplus motor-trucks to men ready to profit by their gratuities, suddenly became a challenger to the rail, and a formidable one. The more sanguine of the new motor hauliers—and some of them were ex-railwaymen with or without grievances—truly believed that they could drive the railway companies out of business in a few years. Converted or unfought bomber aircraft became the world's first air-liners, though their menace was not serious for a long time. But it was the end of the railway monopoly in heavy transport.

All the same, the war had had salutary effects on the international railway industry. As far as the British were concerned, it brought the train ferry into Anglo-Continental operation. Such craft had originated in Scotland, as already noted, in 1850; they had spread to the narrow seas of Scandinavia—where tidal differences were negligible, and to the Great Lakes of North America. War had brought them to the English Channel ports—Southampton and the military port of Richborough, for carrying equipment to France. In 1924 began the public service (for freight only) between Harwich and Zeebrugge. The great tidal differences presented obstacles to scheduled passenger services, which were not to come until the opening of the Dover–Dunkirk ferry in 1936, when for the first time sleeping cars were run nightly between London and Paris. Later, Brussels was to become a second terminal.

Wartime coal shortage in countries with no indigenous supplies imperatively stimulated main-line electrification in Europe. Switzerland and Sweden, with the ready experience of such lines as the Berne–Lötschberg–Simplon and the Lapland iron-ore line (Luleå–Kiruna–Narvik), both made such conversion a matter of national policy. Their example was followed in Italy, Austria, South Germany, and Alpine France. Russian railways, following almost complete breakdown in the revolution and the civil war which followed it, were obsolete and incredibly decrepit. Their rehabilitation was made a primary objective by the Soviets, but it was to be a long business. The Trans-Siberian Railway had been completed before the war, but with a common Russian fault of the time—insufficient capacity over thousands of miles of single track—and had been terribly inadequate for coping with Russia's

Danuvian platform scene, nineteen-twenties; Linz, Austrian Federal Railways, with a Gölsdorf four-cylinder compound engine

Largest of the Beyer-Garratts; Russia ordered her from Gorton Foundry for experimental service, into which she went in 1933

eastern troubles. The nineteen-twenties saw serious work on the provision of new railways in Central Asia, and the Turksib (Turkestan–Siberia) line was completed down to Alma Ata.

There was not much in the way of Russian electrification as yet. Much of the Soviet Union's locomotive stock and vehicles, battered by neglect and war-wrecking, was unworkable, and the old People's Commissariat for Ways and Communications rather wisely ordered immense numbers of new engines to the best of existing designs, such as the well-tried 0–10–0 goods and the famous class Su 2–6–2 passenger engines. Both Sweden and Germany did good business in this market.

Great Western local, *c.* 1920. 'Flower' class engine, heading a mixed assortment

As suggested, the twenty years from 1919 to 1939 saw the first really massive challenge to railway supremacy in heavy transport. Smaller companies faced bankruptcy sooner or later, and as soon as the first of the two German wars was over, consolidation was in the wind. Under the Railways Act of 1921, all British main-line railways were grouped with a view to the formation of several big companies, which could carry the smaller and more indigent lines (such as the Highland Railway) on their backs. Four were formed, and most of the old companies were amalgamated or absorbed into them at the beginning of 1923. The date had been anticipated in a few cases, notably in Wales. One minor main line, the Midland and South Western Junction, kept its independence until the summer of that amalgamation year. The new companies, in order of mileage, were the London Midland and Scottish, the London and North Eastern, the Great Western, and the Southern. Certain jointly owned railways remained as such.

Something of the same kind happened, or had happened, elsewhere in Europe. The old separate State Railways of Germany were amalgamated into the German State Railway Company (*Deutsche Reichsbahn Gesellschaft*); the sometime Dutch State Railways and the Holland Railway were merged, almost imperceptibly at first, into the Netherlands Railways, and so on.

While motor haulage made inroads on both sides of the Atlantic, aircraft were not yet a serious menace to long-distance passenger transport. Flying was a thing to be undertaken out of curiosity, or prestige in some cases, or else extreme and expensive necessity. The private car was already the most menacing rival to the train. It was what a later generation would have called a status symbol. Prestige, therefore, had to be regained by railways on express passenger services by very much higher speeds than had hitherto been considered necessary. Further, a third form of motive power was being cautiously introduced to rail transport.

In the last century compression-ignition oil engines had been made successfully by Herbert Ackroyd-Stuart in England, and improved by Rudolf Diesel in Germany, but at first the oil engine, like the gas engine, was confined to stationary work. Germany and Switzerland furnished the joint cradle of the diesel locomotive, though for some years it was a fractious and ailing child. The first main-line diesel locomotive in the world was built in 1910 by Borsig of Berlin, with a Sulzer (Swiss) engine, and trials took place on the Prussian–Hessian State Railways. With wheel-arrangement 4–4–4, it was driven by a V-shaped low-speed engine with direct drive to a jackshaft in the middle.

Transmission was one of the major problems. Efforts at direct drive, under the influence of steam practice, were frustrating, as in this case. What is quaint is that the idea of electrical transmission—that of an electric locomotive carrying its own power-station on its back—was old. At the end of last century Heilmann had made in France an electric locomotive with a steam-driven generator and electric traction motors. About a decade later Ramsay was producing in Scotland the same sort of electric locomotive with a steam-turbine generator. But in 1924 the Hohenzollern loco-motive works made a workable diesel-electric locomotive for Russia, which naturally was interested in the economic use of oil as fuel, and that was the shape of things to come; though about the same time, and also in Germany, M.A.N. began experiments with a diesel-compressed-air locomotive, outwardly resembling a 4–6–4 steam locomotive with an all-over cab and engine

King George V, Great Western Railway (1927) with the bell presented on a visit to the Baltimore and Ohio Railroad's centennial exhibition

casing instead of a boiler on top, and an enormous radiator in front. Initially there was to be more success with the relatively light train which had a diesel-electric motor car, and this type of train began certain inter-city services both in Germany and in the Middle-Western United States, in the early nineteen-thirties. Memories are short in the States, and it is possible that more Germans today have heard of the *Flying Hamburger* than have Americans of the Union Pacific Railroad's *City of Salina* and the Burlington Route's original *Zephyrs*.

In October 1934 a Union Pacific train averaged 92·1 m.p.h. from North Platte to Alda (129 miles), with a maximum of 120 m.p.h. Previously, on May 26, one of the Burlington *Zephyrs* had run from Denver to Chicago, 1,017 miles, at an average of 77·7 m.p.h.

Steam, as yet, was far from being in retreat, except where there was massive electrification. Just as the first decade of the century had seen great increases in boiler power, aided by superheating, now improvements in the 'front end'—in steam distribution— made the orthodox steam locomotive yet a better machine. Piston valves superseded slide valves. One recalls the work of G. J. Churchward on the Great Western quite early on; he went in for long strokes, long valve-travel and long laps, though when it came to the boiler, he was cautious in providing only a low degree of superheat. Brilliant work was done in France by André Chapelon during the nineteen-thirties; even in the last twilight of steam traction his name remains a legend. On the London Midland and Scottish Railway, Sir William Stanier, who had been one of Churchward's young men, followed Great Western practice, while using bigger boilers, higher pressure and greater superheating surfaces. Sir Nigel Gresley on the London and North Eastern, using very wide grates according to American (and previous Great Northern) practice, and on Pacific type (4–6–2) locomotives, produced some of the fastest passenger engines in regular service. America and Germany, though more given to rather revolutionary experiments, carefully watched these essays in the orthodoxy of locomotive design. There was an outbreak of streamlining in the external portions of steam engines. Some of it was quite spurious, for the word was in fashion, but the work of Stanier, and that of Gresley on the L.N.E.R., certainly assisted by Oliver Bulleid (later of the Southern Railway), was of a very scientific sort. C. F. Dendy Marshall's scholarly work, *The Resistance of Express Trains*, had been published in 1925.

Many of Gresley's locomotives on the L.N.E.R. were three-cylindered, with conjugated valve gear (two sets, with the outside working the inside valves also through rockers.) Normal working pressures were now at various figures in excess of 200 lb. per square inch. The King class on the Great Western (1927 and after) carried 250 lb. per square inch, and, in 1941, Oliver Bulleid used 280 lb. on his new Merchant Navy class Pacifics for the Southern Railway. These last contained Bulleid's very ingenious chain-operated radial valve gear, totally enclosed in an oil-bath, about which mechanical historians will probably argue for as long as steam locomotives are remembered.

Schedules before the outbreak of war were extremely smart under steam traction on several lines in the English-speaking countries, likewise in France, and also in Germany, which had once been of such punctual-pedestrian sort. In the summer of 1933 the Great Western Railway proudly ran *The Fastest Train in the World*, officially the *Cheltenham Flyer*, more baldly the 3.55 p.m. from Swindon to London, with a start-to-stop average of 71·4 m.p.h. for the 77·3 miles. On June 6 of the previous year

On pages 104/105
At King's Cross in the nineteen-twenties, Sir Nigel Gresley's *Flying Scotsman*, one of his original Pacifics, heads the Aberdonian

Top speeds of 100 m.p.h. or over began to occur in public service with Gresley's Silver Jubilee train on the London and North Eastern in 1935

the engine *Tregenna Castle* had made this run with six coaches in 56 minutes 47 seconds, average 81·7 m.p.h., maximum 92·3 m.p.h.

Special fast inter-city services, with streamlined trains, began with the *Silver Jubilee* (London–Newcastle) in 1935, followed by the *Coronation* (London–Edinburgh) and the *Coronation Scot* (London–Glasgow) in 1937. On trial, the latter attained 114 m.p.h. approaching Crewe. Maximum speeds of 126 m.p.h. were attained by Gresley's engine *Mallard* on a braking trial in 1938, near Little Bytham, and by German State engine No. 05.001 on the Berlin–Hamburg line. These will doubtless remain the highest authentic speeds reached with orthodox steam loco-motives. In the United States the Milwaukee company's *Hiawatha* regularly reached 105 m.p.h. in ordinary service. The maximum speed recorded with this train, using 4–6–4 locomotives like the Germans', was 120 m.p.h. But in America, even then, the day of the giant diesel was dawning.

Australian island railway; Tasmanian mail train (3 ft 6 in. gauge) in the nineteen-thirties

In the British Isles, diesel traction began very modestly on the County Donegal Railways in 1931. The giant was still an infant

In the British Isles that day had dawned modestly. In September 1931 the County Donegal Railways put on a little diesel-engined rail-bus, and in December the London and North Eastern had a bogie diesel rail-car, the *Tyneside Venturer*.

It must be admitted that the running of much faster passenger trains was aimed at least in part at restoring a railway image which had been rather slighted by fashion. One remembers from the nineteen-twenties that among the richer bourgeoisie, to travel by train almost entailed loss of caste (except by overnight sleeper). One finds that attitude today among the more affluent proletarians. But there were other very important things.

While North America had had automatic couplings from the end of last century, in Great Britain they were as yet confined on any considerable scale to certain London and North Eastern and Southern Railway stock. But in 1925 the Japanese Government Railways, after years of preparation, made a 24-hours' conversion, surely a record for anything of the kind on such a scale. (Still one remembers with pride, from 1965, the ten-minute replacement of a broken coupler late at night, at Edinburgh Waverley, with the departure made only five minutes late and time quickly made up!)

First class in Spain, 1930. The engine outside is about sixty years older
Author's photomontage; engine by J. E. Kite

Before war broke out in 1939 the Southern Railway had the largest suburban and inter-urban electrified mileage in the world under one management, embracing nearly all of the old London, Brighton and South Coast system and large portions of the South Western and South Eastern, all on 660-volt d.c. This was eventually to lead to almost complete electrification in Southern England from Thanet to the Dorset border.

In freight traffic not only rail-road containers—a very ancient conception but a slow starter—but the use of mechanised marshalling yards made considerable progress. Notable examples of this time were at Hamm in North Germany, on which the yards at Whitemoor in East Anglia were partly modelled, using Thyssen–Fröhlich rail-brakes in conjunction with gravity shunting by hump. 'Humping' on a large scale, however, dated back to 1907, at Wath on the Great Central, where there was heavy traffic from the South Yorkshire coalfield. Probably the largest mechanised

Third class in England, *c*. 1937. The girl's skirt length is the guide!

yard of the nineteen-thirties was that at Markham, on the Illinois Central Railroad in the United States.

The nineteen-thirties saw some notable additions to what may be called the water-gap bridges. The Lower Zambesi Bridge in Portuguese East Africa, 12,064 ft. long, was opened in 1934, two years after the Sydney Harbour Bridge, which, though considerably shorter, has a single arch of 1,650 ft between its approach viaducts. In 1935 came the Huey P. Long Bridge in Louisiana, 23,235 ft long, and at the end of the following year the San Francisco–Oakland Bay Bridge in California, in reality a suspension bridge and a cantilever bridge linked by a tunnel section through an intermediate island; the whole work had a length of 22,720 ft, and included two clear suspension spans of 2,310 ft each. In 1937 the Storstrøm Bridge, 10,537 ft, was completed between Zealand and Falster in the isles of Denmark. A sign of the time was the dual purpose of these bridges, for both railway and road.

In 1945 the old South Station at Vienna lay in ruins. The new one is characteristic of its period. Tramways are not forgotten

Passenger arrangements were considerably improved. Third-class sleeping cars with three superimposed berths had appeared in Sweden as far back as 1910, and their use spread in the nineteen-twenties, first on the German State Railway and then, in 1928, to British railways, where they took the form of four-berth compartments, usually convertible for ordinary day conveyance. North America saw increasing use of compartment sleepers, though the old Pullman arrangement with upper and lower berths flanking a central aisle died hard, and air-conditioned cars were given a welcome.

War, this time expected, broke out in 1939, and once again the British railways came under Government control, though not yet under Government ownership. Once more the railway machine showed its extraordinary adaptability to the sudden conveyance of vast numbers of people and quantities of stores and equipment. From September 1 to 4, 1,399,039 children and expectant mothers were evacuated from the big cities. Most of them later went back, in the absence of immediate heavy bombing, but as the Railway Executive Committee had planned for over twice that number, the movement went very easily. Over half a million were evacuated from London. After the retreat from Dunkirk 620 trains moved 300,000 troops from the Channel ports to dispersal centres about the country. About 10,000 bombs subsequently fell on railway installations. The London and North Eastern was most hit, but the Southern Railway was the more severely damaged, in spite of which it maintained services most nearly approximate to normal schedules. Oil was very precious; private motoring was whittled down to a thread; once again the rails carried the bulk of civil traffic and much military traffic throughout the country. Equipment became worn and, not without precedent, the Government made the best of a hard bargain it had driven with the railway companies.

After the war massive American aid went to the repair of Continental railway systems, many of them devastated, and in the case of the Netherlands Railways, practically destroyed. There was to be little panacea of the kind in Great Britain. In a glow of conscious rectitude Government ownership was instituted as from January 1, 1948. Nine years later a belated plan for modernisation was announced, and that was a signal for various fanatics to

Rapid post-war restoration: Iller Bridges near Kempten, Bavarian Algäu, in 1947

preach their obsolescence and the preferability of letting them rot away in favour of motors. The modernisation was initiated, however, in an attenuated form: the London–Liverpool–Manchester lines, including Birmingham and Stoke, were to be electrified, but not, as had been planned at first, the Great Northern. The very powerful oil interests were pleased by a programme of rapid replacement by diesel locomotives of steam on non-electrified lines; in short, a repetition of what had been happening in the United States, since, as one wit said, 'American railroads sold out to General Motors.' The great virtue of the diesel-electric locomotive (or the diesel-hydraulic locomotive favoured by British Railways, Western Region) is its almost continuous availability

Left Spokane River Bridge, Washington, U.S.A. The east-bound Columbian crosses, still steam-hauled in 1951

Contrast of the nineteen-sixties. The diesel Midland Pullman draws out of Victorian-Gothic St. Pancras, past Victorian-Grecian gas-holder

By night to Scotland, second class

compared with the steam engine, on which many hours are spent in servicing. In this it is the peer of electric locomotives or motor-coaches, without the very heavy capital cost of electrification. The latter, in Great Britain, has so far been justified only by very heavy traffic volumes, for we have not abundant water power.

Of the six Regions of British Railways, the Southern, as might be expected, has electrified with advantage, the area embracing all the south-eastern and central area, together with Hampshire, running eventually as far as Bournemouth. Paradoxically this

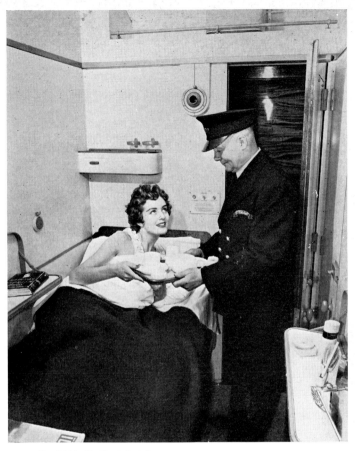

By night to Scotland, first class

nearly-all-electric railway has seen the last regular steam haulage of fast, heavy trains; to Southampton and Bournemouth, pending electrified working. London Midland Regional electrification, accounting for what once were the London and North Western main lines between London and Lancashire, has been noted already. A quite phenomenally successful suburban and inter-urban electrification was carried out in the 'sixties on the Clyde Coast lines of Scottish Region, attracting a pleasantly unexpected wave of public enthusiasm, and custom.

Steam's last winter on the Great Eastern Line, 1962. Conductors are up for the Colchester and Clacton service; diesels are moving in upon the Ipswich and Norwich traffic

Australian inter-city electric multiple-unit train; *The Fish* at Central Station, Sydney

Steam in the small hours. Bristol Temple Meads in the nineteen-fifties

Three levels at Wassen, Gotthard Line, Swiss Federal Railways. The train is the Ticino Trans-Europ-Express from Milan to Zürich

Passing of steam in Russia. What the electric locomotive leaves, the diesel takes, as in much of Western Europe. A 6,000-h.p. diesel by Lugansk Engine Works

On pages 120/121
Diesel trans-continental: *City of Los Angeles*, Union Pacific Railroad

For the rest, the diesel locomotive in one form or another has been the conqueror, and the same sort of thing has happened over much of the world. Oil, for the present, is king.

Railway systems in the older countries have shrunk somewhat, for with the advent of the motor vehicle in its many forms the old country branch line, and the village station on a main line, have become anachronistic. The present mission of railway transport is the provision of heavy, fast surface transport between cities and important towns, and within the suburban perimeters of very large cities. This was the basis in Great Britain of Dr. Richard Beeching's plan to restore viability in a railway industry which, since the war,

119

had become insolvent. The insistence on solvency does not, however, allow for the maintenance of essential railways in remote areas, such as the north-west Highlands of Scotland. While British politicians argued these things, certain other countries, notably vast and sparsely populated Norway, pushed forward railway construction on a fairly grand scale. Russia has continued to take its railways very seriously indeed as a public service, with many grand

Left Unmanned diesels in the middle of a Louisville and Nashville coal train

Three-deck motor-car transport on the Great Northern Railway, USA

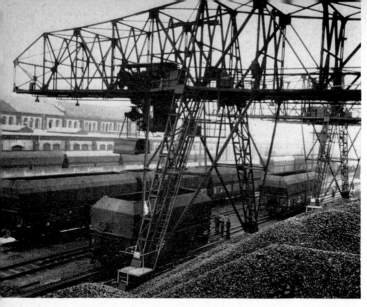

Heavy coal handling at Düsseldorf Power Station

Brunswick, Maryland, in 1952. Mallet freight engine of the Baltimore and Ohio
Railroad heading westbound coal empties ▶

Packing truck-tractor units, Louisville and Nashville Railroad

schemes, including the electrification of the vast Trans-Siberian line. An efficient, disciplined public transport system naturally belongs with a radical political system. American railroads, by contrast, in a free-for-all capitalist society, have been anxious to shed altogether their unremunerative passenger traffic and concentrate on long freight hauls. Citizens—and visitors—especially in the Eastern States, sometimes find this inconvenient. The best of buses is not up to a good train.

Loading aircraft fuel at a German refinery

Modern railway mechanics

So much for current tendencies in railway transport; technical matters deserve a few more notes. In England, Oliver Bulleid on the Southern Railway still aimed at radical improvement of steam traction, unpopular as it had become with business and management circles. His multi-cylinder double-bogie steam locomotive *Leader*, with sleeve valves, a most unusual boiler and other novelties, was a masterpiece of experimental engineering. Had it come earlier in history, it might have taught many profitable lessons and set great precedents. But it was too late and too much of a box-of-tricks for a new State undertaking. Also, Bulleid hated State-planned economies; further, having become Chief Mechanical Engineer of the Southern, he naturally disliked becoming again subordinate through rival seniorities. He became C.M.E. of Coras Iompair Eireann instead, and while at Dublin made remarkable practical experiments in the burning of turf (peat). Again there appeared a double-ended, double-bogie steam locomotive, CC 1, smaller and simpler than the *Leader*, and known to the Irish enginemen as *The Quiet One* for her silence in working. Her firebox was not adequate for turf burning. She would probably have made a good oil-burner, but Bulleid's long working life was at its close. He was 76. Ironically, his parting gift to Ireland's principal railway was heavy diesel power.

With the retreat of steam there has been some work on the gas-turbine locomotive. So far, the Union Pacific Railroad in the States has produced this machine in regular traffic, but in general the diesel continues to hold it own. So does electric traction, where conditions favour it. In 1964 the world's electrified mileage came to 46,707 miles of route, out of a total of 748,719 miles.

Statistics theoretically cannot lie, though they are first-rate things for *suppressio veri* and *suggestio falsi*. This little lot shows nothing of the relative density of traffic on the lines concerned. During the years 1960–63 American railway route mileage decreased by 2,462 miles, from 217,552 to 215,090. The Russians increased theirs from 76,767 to 79,320, that is, by 2,553 route miles. Electrified route mileage was 1,810 in the United States, 1,816 in Great Britain (out of 17,394 miles) and 12,706 in the Soviet Union. The relative percentages are interesting.

Tralee and Dingle, epitomising the now vanished narrow-gauge in Ireland

CPR Mountain Division, 1952. Diesel comes to Lake Louise

Brave New Station! Piccadilly Circus, 1928

130

British standard goods, dividend-earner through eight decades; a Great Eastern example of the nineteen-hundreds, looking for business in the nineteen-fifties

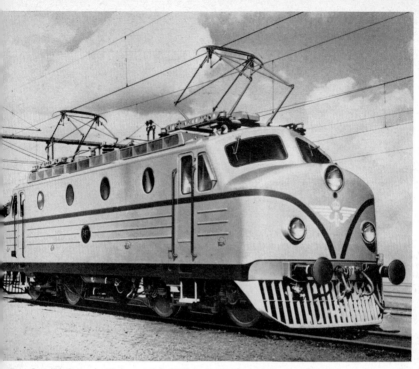

Swedish State electric locomotive, 1955, by Nydqvist and Holm, and A.S.E.A.; 15,000 volts a.c.

Out of a total route mileage of 23,954 in 1963, France had 4,748 miles of route electrified. Out of a relatively small total of 10,328 route miles, Italy had 6,119 miles electrified. In many ways France has been the most interesting country in recent years. Between the wars the then French railway companies had standardised the 1,500-volt d.c. system, with extensive use on the Paris–Orleans–Midi lines. The system was greatly extended, including much of the former Paris, Lyons and Mediterranean Railway, during the nineteen-fifties and early 'sixties. The same system of electric traction was adopted in the Netherlands and Belgium, and in the North of England (e.g. Manchester–Sheffield–Wath, including the new Woodhead Tunnel, 1951–54.) Experimental runs with 1,500-volt d.c. locomotives in the French National Railways' South Western Region produced maximum speeds of 205·6 m.p.h. on two occasions, the present record maximum for orthodox railway vehicles. (Rocket-propelled rail-sledges are *not* orthodox.)

Steam and electric traction, both on the grand scale; Northern Spain, nineteen-sixties

Twenty-five kilovolts. Its first essay between Aix-les-Bains and La-Roche-sur-Foron

Timber train on the Finland State Railways, *c.* 1960. Steam holds out and is, appropriately, wood-fired

Rome Express on the Culoz–Modane mountain section of French National Railways. Series 7100 locomotive 1,500-volt d.c.

Afternoon of Steam; *The Royal Scot* in the middle nineteen-fifties passing King-moor, Carlisle. Engine *Princess Alice*

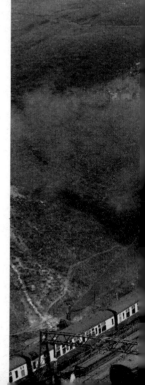

Replacement of Woodhead Tunnels 1954. The new tunnel has never known steam

Over the Pennines. The Manchester–Sheffield–Wath electrification, completed in 1954 with the new Woodhead Tunnel

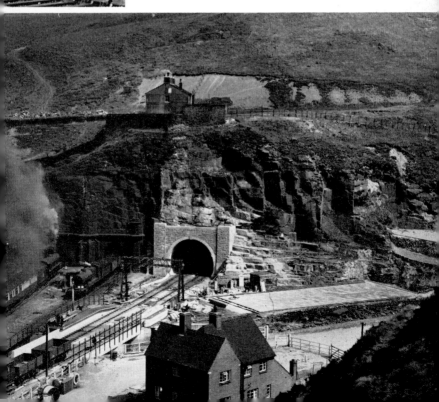

During 1950–51 there was an experimental conversion on the 50-cycle single-phase system, with 25,000 volts at the overhead contact line, over the 48 miles between Aix-les-Bains and La Roche-sur-Foron in Savoy. This system proved to be more economical, following the usual infant ailments, and was extended to many French lines, especially in the North East, and in 1959 was given a trial on the Colchester–Clacton and Walton branches of British Railways' Eastern Region. Further, it was found possible to combine this with 6·25 kV. in city and inner-suburban areas, as was done on the Great Eastern suburban and the London, Tilbury and Southend lines, certain 1,500-volt d.c. lines

1965–66; Achievement of the 25-kilovolt electrification on the primeval London and Birmingham Line

The Gornergrat Railway below the Matterhorn. The line was built with one steam locomotive

of the former being converted. This same 25-kV. system was most importantly adopted from 1960 onwards for the electrification of the former London and North Western lines south of Manchester and Liverpool. With the completion of this to London in 1966, and allowing for the two ferry gaps, it can be said that unbroken electric traction exists on the European railways from Liverpool and Manchester to Syracuse, via Dover and Dunkirk. The systems vary, however. British Railways' Southern Region is faithful to its 660-volt d.c., with third-rail contact; two systems, as already noted, are used in France, and the Italian State Railways, once wedded to three-phase, use 3,000-volt d.c.

Steam and petrol in the Andes; Peruvian Central Railway above the mountain road near San Mateo

America, dominated by oil and motor interests, has seen no important railway electrification since 1938. Russia, on the other hand, has made tremendous progress recently, and adopted the 25-kV. system in 1955.

In the Far East we find the most remarkable development of the mid-twentieth century. Japan is densely populated, very mountainous and has heavy industries. It is therefore a country to which railway transport is more than usually essential. Unfortunately for the Japanese, the country was dowered nearly a century ago with a narrow-gauge railway system (3 ft 6 in.). We should not judge our forebears too severely. To the mid-Victorian technician, Japan was a feudal state, a country out of another

Mechanical snow-shovel, Russia

South from Sydney; Southern Aurora, behind a double-unit diesel-electric locomotive, near Maldon, New South Wales

Commuting to Bombay

world, which could do with some modest railways to help trade
with the rest of the world. The country's later development, for
better or worse, was quite unforeseen when a small British tank
engine with a train of flimsy sun-shaded carriages first toddled
along the 18 miles between Tokyo and Yokohama.

Eventually, and not so very slowly, a very extensive railway network was built, all on 3 ft 6 in. gauge, the same as that of South
Africa and large portions of Australia. By the nineteen-fifties con-
gestion was chronic, above all on the important longitudinal route
known as the Tokaido Line. There were several possibilities; a new
motorway parallel to it, quadrupling of the whole of the existing
line, or the building of an entirely new line, on a larger scale for

through traffic. The second was a matter of make-do-and-mend. The first would favour chiefly the private motorists, who are much less numerous than in the United States. To the surprise of many Western pundits, Japan chose the third and most revolutionary course. Work was begun on the New Tokaido Line in 1959, completion between Tokyo and Osaka being scheduled for the autumn of 1964.

Already the Japanese National Railways were extensively electrified, as well as some company-owned lines, making 5,891 route miles out of a national total of 12,753 miles of route. For the

Beyer-Garratts in Africa; Nairobi sheds, East African Railways and Harbours, in the early nineteen-sixties

The electric signal-box at Waterloo, London, which in 1936 replaced six manual boxes and their innumerable semaphores

Passing of the semaphore : French's balanced arms at Finsbury Park with, below, the colour-lights about to replace them; nineteen-fifties

New Tokaido Line the European standard gauge of 4 ft 8½ in. (1·435 m.) was adopted, with a minimum curve radius of 2,500 metres and heavy-section long welded rails. The line was for inter-city traffic only, in multiple-unit trains, the existing Tokaido Line taking the slower and local traffic. For electric traction the 25-kV. system was adopted with a 60-cycle frequency. There were to be but ten intermediate stations between Tokyo and Shin-Osaka, and the 320 miles, terminal to terminal, were to be covered in three hours by the fastest trains and in four by the others. Initial timetables were to be based on a maximum speed of 120 m.p.h., with automatic train control and centralised traffic control. An experimental section of about 20 miles was completed first and subjected to trials, in the course of which a prototype train reached a top speed of 159 m.p.h.

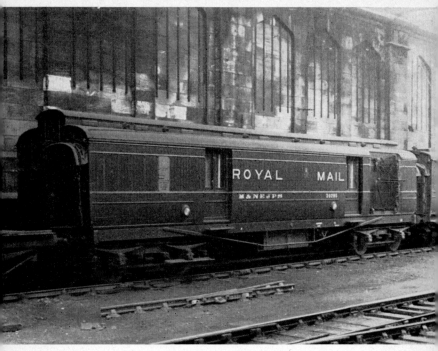

The Travelling Post Office has been with us since 1838. This is a Midland and North Eastern Joint Postal Stock specimen of 1907, still running in 1945

Confronted with this, and with subsequent completion of the scheme, an enthusiast might cry: 'The old railway is dead. Long live the new railway!' But it is not entirely so. The old railway continues to serve many useful purposes in ordinary traffic, while the new one, among other things, offers a very practical alternative to inter-city flying, with its terminal delays and the immense expanses of otherwise useful land needed for airports. Land is not to be wasted in the teeming East! It will be strange, but not to be wondered at, if the real Railway Renaissance is found to have begun in Japan, while Western planners were still arguing as to whether a railway was a commercial undertaking, a public service, or a means of boosting employment.

Heavy transport at very high land speeds needs correspondingly elaborate systems of safeguard, quite apart from the grading and

London and North Western gaslit Travelling Post Office of 1885. There was a unique alternation of fug and draught

Left From the Kenya Highlands, a Beyer-Garratt brings freight down to the port of Mombasa (1964)

On pages 152/153
Strange shapes; Fujiyama broods far above an electric train of the new Tokaido Line, 1965

Last days of steam on the Canadian Pacific, 1950

curvature of the line, which are the main features of motorway construction. Block sections must be longer; high-powered multi-aspect colour-light signals must replace the old semaphores, with automatic control by track circuits. Concentration of signalling over an extensive area on one installation, with the use of electronic equipment where possible, is another recent tendency, speeding up train movements, economising in manpower and reducing greatly the possible pitfalls of divided action. The old ideal of up and down lines, each uni-directional, goes back as we have seen to the beginning of railways—even with horse traction on the Surrey Iron Railway—but with the variable surge of traffic in one direction or the other, there is great advantage in the making of 'reversible' tracks where movements are heavy. From the early nineteen-fifties I recall watching very impressive results north of Dijon in Central France, with three roads, all of which, on the main line from Paris, were made reversible. As one of our senior colleagues remarked at the time: 'When you've been trained to *up* and *down* it gives you a rum feeling to be doing a steady 92 on the wrong road, doesn't it!' We were all used to left-hand running in Great Britain and France, and right-hand running in Germany and the Netherlands, to mention but four, but certainly it was a *rum feeling* on that unprecedented occasion! French railway hospitality was luxurious, however, and after a while we knew that we were quite safe.

This has been but a sketch of a sketch, of a form of heavy land transport that is at once much older than most people think and much more advanced than any other as yet. The motor is a mechanical horse of great merit, ideal for many purposes and which, ironically, was much more enjoyable when it was a rare novelty; it is a machine for transport. The railway is an entire transport machine in itself, ideal for mass movement of freight or passengers, and occupying less space than a motorway of corresponding capacity or, in good flat farming country, a big airport. It is furthermore a disciplined transport machine, peculiarly essential to a fearsomely overpopulated planet. It is not our present intention to discuss whether, sooner or later, both the motor-car and the railway train will vanish before air-cushioned or 'hover' vehicles, or whether the engine in one form or another will give way to motive power by linear induction. Should that become so, the last redoubts of the motive engine will be the ship and the aircraft.

One may remark that with the ultimate vanishing of the engine, the last romance will have gone out of locomotion. It was said with the disappearance of the great sailing ship. It is being said with the disappearance of the noble steam locomotive. It is happening with the jamming of roads by millions of cars, which, by Parkinson's Law, will not be cured by the building of more and more motorways, witness the state of certain American cities today. But the history of technology is full of this sort of thing. Romance simply happens; it cannot be manufactured.

Last ascent of the Rimutaka Incline, New Zealand, 1955, when the present tunnel replaced the Fell centre-rail line

Chronological landmarks

1500s Mining tramways in Central Europe
1727 Causey Arch, Co. Durham
1738 Iron rails in Cumberland
1758 Middleton Railway Act of Parliament
1801 Surrey Iron Railway Act of Parliament
1803 Surrey Iron Railway opened
1804 Trevithick's first railway locomotive
1806 Oystermouth Railway (first passengers)
1812 Steam on the Middleton Railway
1813 Hedley's and Blackett's *Puffing Billy*
1814 George Stephenson's *Blucher* or *My Lord*
1820 Birkinshaw's patent for rolled iron rails
1825 George Stephenson's *Locomotion*
1825 Stockton and Darlington Railway
1827 Hackworth's *Royal George*
1829 George and Robert Stephenson's *Rocket*
1830 Liverpool and Manchester Railway opened (all traffic by steam)
1830 Givors-Rive-de-Gier (Lyons and St. Etienne); first steam line in France
1831 South Carolina Railroad; first regular steam railway in United States
1834 Dublin–Kingstown (Dun Laoghaire); first steam line in Ireland
1835 Brussels–Mechlin; first planned State railway
1835 Nuremberg–Fürth Railway; first German line
1835 First train into Washington (from Baltimore)
1836 London and Greenwich (first London railway)
1836 Festiniog Railway; first public narrow-gauge line
1836 Champlain and St. Lawrence; first line in Canada
1836 Pavlovsk–Tsarskoye Selo; first line in Russia
1837 Grand Junction Railway; first British trunk line
1837 London and Birmingham Railway partly opened; completed in 1838 as first trunk line from London
1838 London and Southampton, and Great Western Railways partly opened; completed to Southampton, and to Bristol, in 1840 and 1841
1839 Amsterdam–Haarlem; first line in Netherlands

1839	Naples–Portici; first Italian line
1841	Electric telegraph block system, Clay Cross Tunnel
1841	Semaphore signals used, New Cross
1842	Edinburgh and Glasgow Railway; first Scottish inter-city line
1845	First mountain tunnel (Woodhead, over 3 miles), England
1846	'Railway Mania'
1846	Interlocked signals, Bricklayers Arms
1848	Completion of West Coast route, London–Glasgow and Edinburgh
1848	Barcelona–Mataro; first line in Spain
1848	Great Western record run to Didcot; 67 m.p.h. average
1849	High-Level Bridge, Newcastle
1850	Britannia Bridge, Menai Straits
1850	Royal Border Bridge
1850	Forth and Tay train ferries
1850	Nicholson's compounding experiment, Eastern Counties Railway
1850	Great Northern Railway completed East Coast Route
1850	South Wales Railway, Chepstow to Swansea
1853	Bombay–Thana; first line in India
1853	Staff system for single track
1854	First lines in Brazil, Norway and Australia
1855	Beattie's feedwater heater
1856	Grand Trunk Railway, Montreal–Toronto
1856	Saxby's complete interlocking of signals and points
1856	First lines of Swedish State Railways
1856	Lisbon–Carregado; first line in Portugal
1857	Parque–Floresta; first line in Argentina
1857	First steel rail, by R. F. Mushet; Derby
1859	Royal Albert Bridge, Saltash
1859	First (improvised) Pullman sleeping car, USA
1859	Giffard's injector used on locomotives
1860	Natal Railway; first in South Africa
1860	Ramsbottom's locomotive water-pickup
1863	Metropolitan Railway; first city underground line
1863	Christchurch–Ferrymead; first steam line in New Zealand
1865	Colombo–Ambepussa; first in Ceylon
1865	Pullman's first new car, USA
1868	Fell's Mont Cenis Railway
1869	First important flyover junction (Birdswood, London and North Western Railway)

1869 American trans-continental line completed

1870 Tower Subway, with cable tram; world's first tube line

1871 Col de Frejus (Mont Cenis); first long Alpine tunnel

1872 Yokohama–Yedo (Tokio); first line in Japan

1873 First British sleeping cars

1874 Pullman cars imported by Midland Railway from the United States

1878 Bouch's Tay Bridge (destroyed in 1879)

1879 Berlin; first (exhibition) electric line

1881 Berlin–Lichterfelde; world's first public electric line

1881 London–Brighton; first electric train-lighting

1882 St. Gotthard Tunnel

1883 Magnus Volk in Brighton; first English electric line

1883 Giant's Causeway, Ireland; first hydro-electric-powered line

1884 Belgrade–Nish: first line in present Jugo-Slavia

1885 West Coast Special Travelling Post Office (no passengers)

1885 Alloa Bridge, with swing-span, across Firth of Forth

1885 Canadian Pacific Railway; lines joined from Montreal to the Pacific Coast (first through train, 1886)

1886 Severn Tunnel; longest in the world under water

1887 The Barlows' Tay Bridge (see 1878)

1889 Continuous automatic brakes made compulsory in the United Kingdom

1890 Fowler's and Baker's Forth Bridge

1890 London; world's first electric tube line

1893 Liverpool; world's first electric elevated railway

1893 112·5 m.p.h. on the New York Central

1895 Electric main-line haulage, Baltimore Belt Line, U.S.A.

1898 Prussia; Schmidt's smoke-tube superheater

1899 Great Central; last main line into London

1903 Mersey Railway; first electrification of steam underground, (London Metropolitan and District lines followed in 1905)

1906 Automatic warning (cab signals) Great Western Railway; extended 1908 and after

1906 First Simplon Tunnel

1909 South London; beginning of Southern electric network

1910 Borsig–Sulzer diesel locomotive

1910 Trans-Andine line completed; Argentine–Chile

1913 Berne–Lötschberg–Simplon Railway, 15-kV single-phase

1917 Trans-Australian Railway

1923 Four British railway companies formed out of 123